MW00396362

Music is my life and my life is music.
-Mozart

TrantBooks

MUSIC NOTATION GUIDE

STAFF
- The Staff (or Stave) is made up of five horizontal lines that are numbered from bottom to top
- The bottom line is the First Line and the top line is the Fifth Line
- Each line and space on the Staff represents a different musical pitch or tone
- Music is written on the lines and in the spaces of the Staff

GRAND STAFF
- When two staves are joined together it is called a Grand Staff or Great Stave

Treble Clef
- The top staff/stave is called the Treble Clef

Bass Clef
- The bottom staff/stave is called the Bass Clef

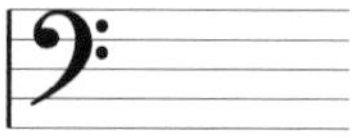

- In piano, the right hand plays the Treble Clef and the left hand plays the Bass Clef

BARS AND BAR LINES
- The vertical lines on the staff/stave are called Bar Lines
- The spaces in between the Bar Lines are called Bars
- Two vertical lines are called a Double Bar Line
- The Double Bar Line means the end of the piece or section of music

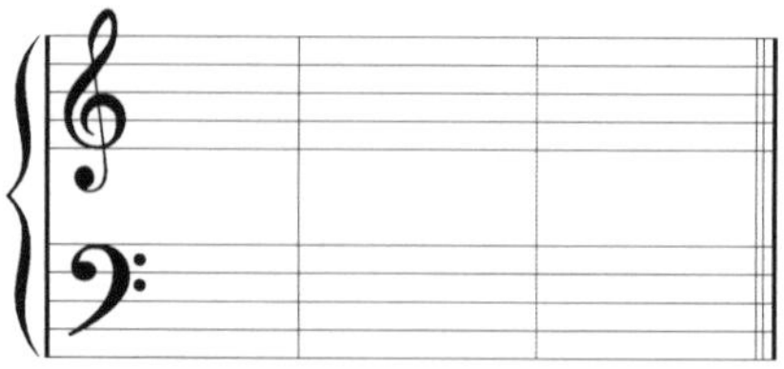

TIME SIGNATURES
- The top number shows the number of beats per Bar
- The bottom number shows the type of Note being counted

4 quarter notes per bar

6 eighth notes per bar

NOTES

- Notes (or keys) are placed on the lines and in the spaces of the Staff

- There are seven letters used for music notes

A B C D E F G

Treble Clef Line Notes

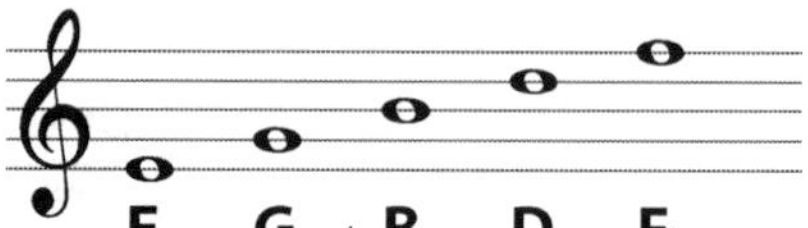

Every **G**ood **B**oy **D**oes **F**ine

Bass Clef Line Notes

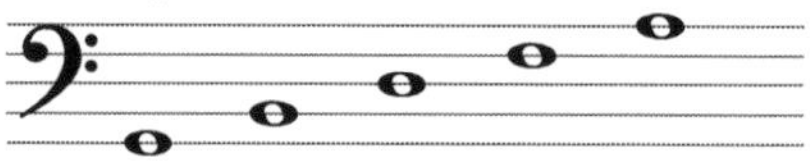

Great **B**ig **D**ogs **F**all **A**sleep

Treble Clef Space Notes

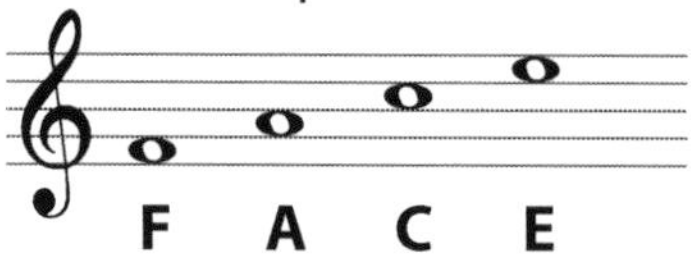

F A C E

Bass Clef Space Notes

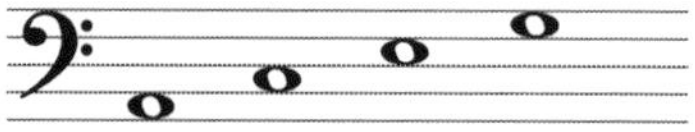

All **C**ows **E**at **G**rass

SYMBOL	NOTE (4/4 Time)
	Whole Note (Play for 4 beats)
	Half Note (Play for 2 beats)
	Quarter Note (Play for 1 beat)
	Eighth Note (Play for 1/2 a beat)
	Sixteenth Note (Play for 1/4 beat)

RESTS

- Silence in music is represented by Rest symbols

SYMBOL	REST (4/4 Time)
	Whole Rest (Rest for 4 beats)
	Half Rest (Rest for 2 beats)
	Quarter Rest (Rest for 1 beat)
	Eighth Rest (Rest for 1/2 a beat)
	Sixteenth Rest (Rest for 1/4 beat)

DID YOU KNOW
In American English "Staff" is more commonly used and in British English it's "Stave". In both cases the plural is "Staves".

Manufactured by Amazon.ca
Bolton, ON

12740394R00057